EMOTIONAL ATTACHMENT

Unlock the Secrets to a Lasting and Fulfilling Relationship

John K. Betts

Table of contents

Introduction

The concept of emotional attachment is integral to our humanity. It is the ability to form strong bonds and connections with others and to feel deeply for them. It is an essential part of our existence and something that shapes the way we live our lives. From the very first moment of life, we are searching for a sense of belonging and connection, and over time these connections develop into strong emotional attachments. Through these attachments, we can experience joy, love, comfort, security, and support. Emotional attachment can be powerful and sustaining, and it can help us to build a strong foundation for our lives.

Our emotional attachments—the deep and meaningful connections we share with others are essential to our physical, mental, and spiritual health. They are the foundation of our existence, allowing us to experience joy, security, love, and peace. No matter our age, race, gender, or background, we all crave emotional attachments. We often feel an ebb and flow of emotion, relying on the people we love and trust to buoy us in tougher times and celebrate with us when things go well. Our emotional attachments are an integral part of our life and the way we interact and form relationships with the people around us. Emotional attachments can be tricky to define, as they are not always easy to explain. We don't always know why we feel a certain way toward someone, and the depth and intensity of our attachment can vary over time. Simply put, an emotional attachment is when we deeply care about someone, when we love and feel a strong connection with another person. It can be a close friend, family member, romantic partner, or even a pet.

The quality of emotional attachment is essential in our relationships, as it implies a genuine caring for the other person that goes beyond shallow or simply physical connections. We rely on our emotional attachments to feel safe, secure, and fulfilled, and it is up to us to foster and nourish them.

Making a conscious effort to nurture your emotional attachments can be immensely fulfilling. Being open and honest about your feelings, finding ways to express yourself, connecting deeply with people, and being vulnerable are all ways to instantly boost your emotional connections. Regular self-reflection can help you pinpoint the connections that matter to you the most so that you can put in the effort to build on them. Focusing on positive communication, expressing gratitude, and exploring active listening techniques are other great ways to improve your emotional attachment with others.

Ultimately, emotional attachments are the lifeblood of a meaningful life. By caring, supporting, and understanding each other, we can grow relationships that provide love, joy, security, and companionship—all essential in creating a life full of beauty and purpose.

Chapter 1

Understanding Emotional Attachment

Emotional attachment is the bond created between two people that shares an emotional connection. It involves the exchange of feelings, experiences, and support. An emotional attachment is not necessarily restricted to being between two people in a romantic relationship, as it can be found in platonic relationships as well.

When two people form an emotional attachment they become connected on an intimate level; they share a bond of trust, understanding, empathy, and compassion. They listen to each other and actively strive to meet each other's needs. They become a team, and often their lives become intertwined. Emotional attachment is a type of psychological connectedness, and it is often accompanied by feelings of intimacy, attachment, and infatuation. It is important to understand that emotional attachment can be a positive thing. It offers security and comfort to both parties involved. It can bring a sense of stability and companionship to a relationship, and it can generate mutual feelings of joy and fulfillment. It is important, however, to remember that emotional attachment requires time and effort to sustain it. Without effort, the connection made could start to weaken or fade. Emotional attachment is vital for long and healthy relationships. It is necessary for trust, respect, and understanding, and it is an integral element of a well-rounded relationship. Without emotional attachment, relationships can feel distant and strained. To nurture a relationship, it is essential to

invest effort into growing and maintaining
emotional attachment.

Signs of Emotional Attachment

Emotional attachment is the bond between two
people that draws them closer together and often
creates a sense of belonging in the relationship.
Signs of emotional attachment can vary from person
to person, but can generally include feelings of
security, comfort, trust, and care within the
relationship.

Signs of emotional attachment include expressing a
desire to be physically close, wanting to make plans
with one another, confiding in each other, sharing
secrets, being able to express positive and negative
feelings without fear of judgment, enjoying shared

social activities, sharing responsibilities, offering
support, and being available when needed.

It is also common in emotionally attached
relationships to feel a sense of loss when apart, to be
excited to see one another, to look forward to being
together, and to think of the other person often. If a
relationship has these characteristics, it can be a sign
of emotional attachment.

However, emotional attachment is not always
positive and can lead to feelings of jealousy,
possessiveness, and insecurity. If you are in a
relationship and these types of behaviors arise, it
could be a sign that you are too emotionally attached
and are not setting healthy boundaries in the
relationship.

Benefits of Emotional Attachment

Emotional attachment is a powerful bond between two people or a person and an animal. Studies show that having a strong emotional attachment can be beneficial in one's life.

1) Increased Sense of Security: A strong emotional attachment provides a sense of security and stability in life. Studies have shown that a close emotional attachment provides a haven for people during times of difficulty, allowing them to cope better with life's challenges.

2) Increased Self-Esteem: Building a strong emotional bond with another can offer people a confidence boost. That sense of being seen and appreciated will provide a feeling of worth, leading to increased self-esteem and self-love.

3) Higher Happiness Levels: Developing a strong emotional bond with someone can increase happiness levels. Being in a relationship with someone who deeply cares for you can provide an emotional outlet, leading to improved moods and less stress.

4) Improved Mental Well-being: A strong emotional connection can help to reduce anxiety and depression. Having someone to talk to, to confide in, and to lean on can be invaluable in one's journey to mental well-being.

All in all, having an emotional attachment can help you lead a happy and fulfilled life, whether it be between two people or a person and an animal. Being able to express your emotions openly in a healthy relationship, in which unconditional love is present, can help to keep the loneliness away. It is

important to take care of mental health and
emotional attachment can be a great way to do this.

Chapter 2

Attachment Theory

Attachment theory is an area of psychology that examines the emotions and the psychological patterns of attachment that exist between human beings. It is studied by developmental psychologists, social psychologists, and evolutionary biologists, and it is primarily focused on the relationships and bonds that exist between an infant and their primary caregiver.

Attachment theory was first proposed in the 1940s by British Psychoanalyst John Bowlby to explain the bonding and emotional connection between an infant and their primary caregiver. He suggested that the quality of these interactions has a significant impact on development throughout later life and influences how individuals cope with various emotions and form relationships. The theory focuses on three main components; secure attachment, insecure attachment, and disorganized attachment.

Secure attachment occurs when the baby has formed an emotional connection with their primary caregiver and can survive with a sense of security, trust, and independence. This secure attachment allows the child to form a close and loving bond with the caregiver and this emotional connection can help to facilitate healthy psychological development.

Insecure attachment occurs when an infant experiences inconsistent or insensitive caregiving. This can lead to an unhealthy attachment with their primary caregiver and can cause insecurity, mistrust, and a fear of abandonment.

Disorganized attachment occurs when the infant has no clear attachment pattern and the relationship speaks out of societal norms such as abuse or neglect and creates an overwhelming fear or confusion in the child.

Attachment theory has shed light on the importance of the needs of children and how they are supported as they grow. It helps to inform the work of parenting and caretaking and is an essential element in guiding and supporting the development of healthy attachments in children.

The Four Major Attachment Styles

The four major attachment styles are,

- Secure Attachment
- Anxious-Ambivalent Attachment
- Avoidant Attachment
- Disorganised Attachment

Secure Attachment Style: This is a style of attachment involving a sense of trust and security in relationships. Those who have a secure attachment style feel secure in their relationships and are willing to express their needs to their partner. They are responsive and reciprocal in the way they express their feelings. They can handle disagreements and conflict healthily and maturely.

Anxious-Ambivalent Attachment Style: This type of attachment is characterized by an intense need to be close to a partner despite feeling insecure and uncomfortable in the relationship. They tend to have an anxious view of relationships, fearing being abandoned and feeling anxious when a partner is not around. In addition, they tend to often feel jealous and possessive as well as constantly needing reassurance and requesting more closeness than their partner can provide.

Avoidant Attachment Style: This type of attachment is marked by a fear of closeness and intimacy. People who have an avoidant attachment style tend to keep their distance and can be unwilling to open up and share thoughts and feelings. They may distance themselves emotionally and prefer to not engage in deeper conversations and activities. Instead, they may use words or actions that prevent the other person from getting too close.

Disorganized Attachment Style: This type of attachment involves feeling fragmented and uncertain in relationships. People with a disorganized attachment style may avoid intimate closeness and yet experience intense anxiety when apart from their partner. They may be inconsistent in their interactions, often feeling confused and overwhelmed. They may also have difficulty regulating their emotions and handling conflict. This attachment style is likely the result of early childhood experiences in a chaotic or neglectful environment.

Chapter 3

How to create a secure attachment

Creating a secure attachment with your partner is essential for the success of any relationship. To create a secure attachment with your partner, it is important to focus on empathy, communication, and open dialogue.

The first step in creating a secure attachment is to practice empathy. Empathy involves actively understanding and caring for your partner's feelings and needs. To build empathy, try to relate to your partner by understanding what they are feeling and expressing your own understanding and emotional support.

It is also important to practice good communication with your partner. This includes being honest and open about your feelings and being willing to discuss and resolve conflicts together. Work on listening to each other and remaining present at the moment to work through issues together.

You should also strive to create an environment of openness and dialogue. Share your thoughts and feelings with your partner and be open to hearing their thoughts and feelings in return. Encourage constructive and open dialogue to come to a better understanding and resolution of any issues or conflicts.

Finally, make sure to express your love and support for your partner by taking an active interest in their life and letting them know that you love them. Show your love through physical and verbal affection, and remind each other of why you are together and how important it is to you. By establishing a strong emotional connection through empathy, communication, and open dialogue, you can create a secure attachment with your partner.

Creating attachment Bonds with others

Creating an attachment bond with others is one of the most important and meaningful elements of building relationships. It can be built through a variety of activities such as spending quality time with them, sharing emotions and feelings, and simply being an active and reliable listener.

First and foremost, forming an attachment bond is about making a genuine effort to invest in the relationship. Quality time spent together, whether it's having a cup of coffee, going for a walk, or reading a book together, is essential in building the bond. By

simply being in each other's company, meaningful conversations will naturally occur that help establish trust and understanding between the two parties. Moreover, opening up about your emotions and feelings can be a powerful tool in creating an attachment bond. Putting yourself in a vulnerable state and giving the other person the chance to see your softer side can create an openness that engenders trust and strengthens your connection. Finally, being an active listener is the cornerstone of building an attachment bond. A lack of judgment and genuine interest in what the other person has to say will demonstrate that you value them and their thoughts. As a result, they will both feel heard and be more likely to express themselves openly and honestly in the future.

Ultimately, creating an attachment bond with others is an invaluable way to build meaningful relationships and take them to the next level. By

investing time and energy into the relationship, and being an active listener, you can develop a deep and lasting connection that will last for many years to come.

Understanding Attachment Behaviours

Attachment behaviors refer to how individuals interact, bond, and express love with one another in interpersonal relationships. These behaviors are commonly observed in romantic relationships, though they can also be seen between parents and children, siblings, and other close relationships. Attachment behaviors involve a person providing a sense of security and safety to their partner, seeking approval or validation, and feeling connected and secure in their relationships.

Attachment behaviors are thought to have a great impact on the development of relationships and the emotional health of individuals. Secure attachment behavior is associated with higher levels of communication, satisfaction, and stability in relationships. People with secure attachment styles are more comfortable with emotions, have better social skills, and are less likely to experience depression, anxiety, and low self-esteem. Conversely, more insecure attachment styles can lead to distress and difficulties in relationships. It is important to understand attachment behaviors to provide necessary support in close relationships. Practicing healthy communication is one way to encourage secure attachment behavior and build strong relationships. Open and honest dialogue, active listening, self-disclosure, and validating one

another are all ways to foster an environment of

connection and security. It is also important to build

boundaries and recognize when lines are crossed and

communication is not productive.

Ultimately, understanding attachment behaviors will

enable individuals to develop loving, secure, and

fulfilling relationships. This allows individuals to

receive the comfort and support that they need to

feel connected and secure in their relationships and

to experience overall emotional well-being.

Chapter 4

How to Manage Difficult Emotions

Managing difficult emotions can be a daunting task, especially when those emotions are deep, intense, and threaten to overwhelm. It is possible to control these emotions, nevertheless, in a healthy way.

Here are some tips for managing difficult emotions:

1. Recognize what you are feeling. The first step in managing difficult emotions is to recognize what emotion you are feeling. Pay attention to your body and become aware of such physical sensations as tightness in your chest or throat, butterflies in your stomach, trembling hands, or a sinking feeling in the

pit of your stomach. These physical sensations might provide clues as to what emotion you might be feeling.

2. Accept the emotion. Instead of trying to deny or suppress the emotion, try acknowledging that the emotion exists and accept that it is part of you. Allow yourself to feel the emotion without judgment and self-criticism.

3. Talk to someone. Talking to someone who is not directly involved in the situation can help you manage and process your difficult emotions.

4. Write about it. It can be relieving to write about your feelings. It can help you to work through the emotion and understand it better.

5. Make use of grounding techniques.
Grounding techniques are designed to help bring

you into the present and can help prevent or limit emotional overwhelm. These might include mindfulness meditation, deep breathing, going for a short walk

and focusing on the details of your environment, or engaging in some creative activity such as writing, painting, or playing music.

6. Exercise. Exercise can be a powerful way to manage difficult emotions by channeling energy and tapping into the feel-good hormones, and endorphins released in the body during exercise.

7. Remember that it will pass. Most difficult emotions are temporary and can be managed if given enough time. Know that by taking the above steps, emotions will eventually pass, and you will eventually feel better.

Identifying and Labeling Emotions

Identifying and labeling emotions is an important life skill. It aids in our understanding of both ourselves and those around us. It may also help us manage our emotions and behavior better. Learning how to identify and label emotions starts with recognizing our feelings. It is also important to reflect on how our emotions impact us, how they may guide our decisions or behavior, and how they may affect the people around us.

Once we have identified our emotions, it's important to label them. Labeling emotions gives us the

language to talk more accurately and specifically
about our feelings and helps us to better process and

respond to them. Labeling an emotion can also help
us think more critically about our feelings and
recognize what underlying needs we need to take
care of.

When we can accurately identify and label our
emotions, it can have a positive impact on our
mental health. It can also equip us with the skills to
better communicate our emotions to others, which is
essential in maintaining strong and healthy
relationships. It is important to note that labeling
emotions can be difficult and tricky at times. It may
take time and practice to become more aware and
proficient at it.

Coping with Difficult Emotions

Coping with difficult emotions can be a daunting yet rewarding process. It is important to recognize that it is okay to feel emotion, no matter how uncomfortable it may be. It is essential to recognize the emotion(s) you are experiencing and why you are feeling that way to effectively work through it. When it comes to difficult emotions, it is helpful to practice self-compassion and to recognize that sometimes unhealthy behaviors or reactions are just automatic responses to a given situation. Instead of allowing yourself to be consumed by the emotion, take a few moments to name the feeling, note its intensity, and take a deep breath.

Another helpful coping technique is mindfulness. Mindfulness is the practice of focusing on the present moment without judgment or attempts to change the emotion. This can help to create distance between your present moment and the initial emotion or thought that caused it. Once you have acknowledged and accepted the feeling without judgment, you can move forward to problem-solve or create a plan to cope with the emotion healthily. Finally, it can be beneficial to rely on social support to cope with difficult emotions. Reaching out to close loved ones, a therapist or a support group can provide an outlet to discuss and process those feelings in a secure environment.

No matter how difficult a feeling may be, it is possible to find a way through it with the help of self-care and support. It's important to remember that it is okay to not be okay and to take the time to work through difficult emotions as part of your self-care routine.

Conclusion

Emotional attachment is an important part of life. Its presence in our relationships can foster a sense of comfort, security, and trust. Without it, relationships may become disconnected or even break down completely. We must recognize the importance of emotional connections and take steps to nurture and strengthen them. This can be done through communication, spending quality time together, expressing affection, and actively listening to and validating each other. Emotional attachment is both beneficial and worthwhile and can result in healthier, richer, and more fulfilling relationships. Finally, it is vital to remember that emotional attachment is an ongoing process that needs to be maintained and nurtured to keep it strong. It will

take effort and understanding, but the rewards are
worth it.

www.ingramcontent.com/pod-product-compliance
Lightning Source LLC
Chambersburg PA
CBHW051900250726
48659CB00006B/2327